SAFE TO GROW

**Guidelines on child protection
for the local church and its youth workers**

**Prepared by the Children's Working Group
of the Baptist Union of Great Britain
Chaired by the Revd Anne Dunkley**

**Published by
The Baptist Union of Great Britain**

Illustrations by Linda Francis

Printed by Stanley Hunt Printers Ltd, Rushden, Northants

SAFE TO GROW

Contents

Foreword

I wish that *Safe to Grow* did not need to be published, but in these days of social change and shifting moral values, parents entrust their children to us for nurture, safe care and wise leadership. It is a sad fact that amongst Christian people, as in the wider society children can be hurt. So in our children's and youth work we cannot be satisfied until we are sure we have done all in our power to protect them from harm of all kinds.

This publication is a major step towards recognising the care which needs to be taken when working with children. The Children's Working Group raises important issues and makes practical suggestions. *Safe to Grow* is both comprehensive and wide-ranging, and I believe that it should be essential reading in every Baptist church for those who devote themselves to the nurture of children and young people.

The passing of the Children Act in 1989 was a landmark in promoting good, safe practice in long-term child care, to be followed in 1993 by the Code of Practice, *Safe from Harm*, which aims to help voluntary organisations working for shorter periods with children and young people. To put into practice the thirteen principles of *Safe from Harm* appears daunting and may seem to call into question the integrity of our children's and youth workers. *Safe to Grow*, the Baptist Union's response to the government recommendations, shows neither to be the case. It makes the guidelines accessible to every church, providing a framework which can be adapted to individual situations. It has been written in consultation with children's and youth workers, ministers, social workers, survivors of abuse, and the solicitor of the Baptist Union.

As we commit ourselves in our churches to the adoption of these guidelines, we are making a positive contribution to the safe growth of children and young people in the life God intends them to enjoy.

David Coffey
General Secretary   November 1994

Clarification of terms:

Titles used within churches vary. For the purposes of this booklet, a **worker** is anyone who is engaged in children's or young people's work on the church's behalf. A **leader** is anyone who has a supervisory, organisational or decision-making role. Workers and leaders may be in any group belonging to the church, including the uniformed organisations.

Where either 'children' or 'young people' are mentioned in the text, both are intended.

Although *Safe from Harm* gives recommendations for the care of young people under 16, the definition of a child under the Children Act 1989 is a person under 18. To promote best practice, we are adopting the latter definition.

Introduction

Why this booklet?

Sarah is crying as she comes to church. Has she fallen over, has her hamster died? As her 'Junior Church' worker, you listen to her problems. What she tells you indicates that she is being abused at home.

Matthew is crying as he leaves church. Has he hurt himself, has his birthday been forgotten? As his youth group leader, you listen to his problems. What he tells you suggests that one of the other youth workers may be abusing him.

Today, scenes like these could take place in any one of our churches.

Today, we have to recognise the fact that some children and young people are abused physically, emotionally, sexually or by neglect.

They may come to us bearing the marks of this abuse from their own unsafe world.

Churches work safely and responsibly with millions of children and young people, but just occasionally those who have been entrusted to work with them may cause them harm.

The Home Office has produced a set of Recommendations and Guidelines to give all voluntary groups, including churches, a framework for action to promote children's welfare, in particular to prevent abuse taking place. Called *Safe from Harm*, (Pub: Home Office, London 1993, ISBN 0 862529 93-X) the Recommendations and Guidelines do not have the force of law, but recommend the steps which should be taken to safeguard everyone under 18.

Churches hold a trusted position in the community. We will be expected to follow the recommendations so that all who work with children and young people, as well as the church's leaders, know how to:

- protect them from abuse;
- act responsibly if abuse is discovered or disclosed.

This booklet has been written to give churches and their leaders the guidance they need to follow the guidelines and to keep our children safe - SAFE TO GROW.

Myths ...   **"It couldn't happen here"**
"We don't have enough children to bother about it"
"We're desperate for helpers; anyone who offers is welcomed warmly"

... which have been exploded   **In 1990, almost 44,000 children were registered as 'at risk'**
Any child *could* be abused; any adult *could* be an abuser;
Child abusers are devious and may be drawn to places where they have easy access to children.

How to use SAFE TO GROW

The purpose of this booklet is to give you a way in to adopting the good practice which the government recommendations contain. We recommend that you use it to draw up:

1. A **policy statement** in which your church commits itself to the safe care and growth of children, and resolves to follow the Home Office Recommendations *Safe from Harm*;

    and

2. A **good practice guideline**, and **procedures**, as set out in the appendices to this booklet.

The booklet helps you through every stage. Taking as our starting point the biblical base for proper care of children and young people, we then acknowledge that we live in a fallen world where they are sometimes in danger. The different ways in which they can be harmed are described. The remainder of the booklet gives advice about preparing for, dealing with and preventing incidents of abuse, in accordance with the Guidelines.

Further help is available from many sources. A list of agencies you can turn to for advice or training appears in Appendix 6, p 39. The Baptist Youth Ministry Office can also offer some guidance - their address can also be found in Appendix 6.

You may find while using this booklet that your church is thinking and talking about children and young people in a different way. Perhaps you will question some of your assumptions about the way you journey together as the household of God made up of people of all ages. To help you to seize this opportunity and review your patterns of life, learning and worship, some suggestions are given which may help you on the road ahead.

Children and young people in God's world and in his church

All human beings are made by God in his image. The image of God is his gift to us in childhood as well as in adulthood. In our fallen world, his image has become marred.

The story of God's people tells us how they strayed from his design. God called many to speak his word afresh to succeeding generations in Israel; among them were Samuel and Jeremiah, both in their youth (1 Sam 3, Jer 1:4-8). When Jeremiah tried to use his age as an excuse, God chided him: "'Do not say, I am only a child." ' .

Jesus' birth, and his growth and nurture within a family, affirm the dignity and value conferred by God on children and young people. God's experience of childhood is a part of the process of our salvation, finished in the adult life and death he knew in Jesus. A child is a whole person with rights and needs, to be honoured and respected by us all. Indeed children possess qualities which show adults the way to God's kingdom (Matt 18:3).

So children are valued yet vulnerable members of the Christian community, who need our special care. We take seriously the charge given by Jesus to welcome children (Luke 9:48), to protect them (Matt 18:6-10) and to allow them free access to him (Mark 10:13-16).

Churches today have a unique opportunity to enact these commands of Jesus, and to stand with children and young people in the face of a culture which still regards them as possessions. Every church should model in its worship, fellowship and mission a community where:

● children are listened to, given a sense of belonging, nurtured, and kept safe;
● parents are supported and encouraged;
● those who work with children and young people are supported and protected.

Sadly, child abuse is not something new. When we read the curse against children at the end of Psalm 137, we realise how deep-rooted is the desire to hurt them. But it is only gradually during this century that abuse, particularly sexual abuse, has been recognised, named and condemned. The protection of children from harm has now become a real issue because recent cases have received wide publcity. As a consequence many adults who suffered secretly in their own childhood feel able for the first time to explore the pain and the grief of what happened to them, and to seek help. The pastoral care which can be given to survivors is described on p 15.

How can children be harmed?

When children and young people receive loving care and discipline (against which they sometimes rebel!) in a safe environment they have every chance to grow into healthy stable adulthood. They can be prevented from growing and developing normally by adults or by other children who do wrong things to them. Damage of this kind is termed 'abuse'.

Children who suffer abuse will behave in a variety of abnormal ways as they struggle to cope with a world that is going wrong for them.

Workers with children and young people need to be able to detect the signs, because they are the cries for help which, in most cases, cannot or dare not be articulated.

However, there may be other reasons for what a child is doing, and a worker must never be required to take a decision on her or his own as to whether abuse is taking place. The church must agree and publicise a process of consultation and of action if abuse is suspected, as recommended in Guideline 12. Appendix 4, p 30, has an example of a list of procedures which can be given to workers.

How might a child suffer abuse?

There are several categories of abuse officially defined in government documents. Of these the following are the most common:

physical abuse,
where children's bodies are hurt or injured;

emotional abuse,
where children don't receive love and affection, may be frightened by threats and taunts, or are given responsibilities beyond their years;

sexual abuse,
where adults will use children and young people to satisfy sexual desires; other children can also be abusers.

neglect,
where adults persistently and severely fail to care for children and protect them from danger, leading to serious impairment of the child's health or development

A variety of personal circumstances can cause adults to abuse children physically or to neglect them. These kinds of abuse may be easier to detect. Signs of emotional and sexual abuse are very difficult to spot. With sexual abuse in particular, secrecy imposed by the offending adult is part of the abuse pattern, so the child will not readily disclose what is happening.

A summary of signs of abuse is given in Appendix 4, p 30.

Who abuses children?

- An abuser is most often someone known to the child. It may be a parent, sibling, other relation, family friend or neighbour.
- Sometimes, the abuser may be an adult who holds a position of authority over children, as in a church.
- They can be people of any background.
- There is no certain way of identifying a would-be abuser; they don't appear different from the rest of society.
- They are people who are themselves in desperate need and require help.
- Many adult abusers have been abused themselves as children.

**The church may have a significant role of pastoral care for the abuser, and those close to him or her.
But the primary concern is always the safety of the child.**

Training our workers to help an abused child

Workers' feelings

Most of the government's Guidelines are concerned with good practice to protect children. When you implement the Guidelines, you are helping to prevent abuse taking place in church-based life.

But as you adopt the recommendations, your leaders and workers will be preparing to face distressing situations. Some of them may be inexperienced young adults. All may need help in coping with their feelings about child abuse.

Through careful training, workers can be helped to handle their emotions before they meet a 'real-life' case of abuse. If a child begins to tell their secret to a worker who, being unprepared, shows revulsion to what is being disclosed, the child can feel guilty. The victim needs to talk to someone who is not visibly shocked, but who will accept attentively what is being said. Appendix 4, p 30, gives a list of procedures.

Defence mechanisms

We are often reluctant to admit abuse is taking place, especially **to** children whose families we may know, or **by** people we trust. We have an unconscious defence mechanism which refuses to see abuse. All this is natural. But it must never prevent us from keeping alert to its possibility. This is not the same as treating everyone with suspicion. Training helps to place all this in perspective.

Other help

There are many agencies through which training can be set up, according to your church's circumstances. There may be a trained and experienced member of your own or a neighbouring church who would do it. Other organisations to approach are listed in Appendix 6, p 39. Voluntary bodies will usually have to charge a fee, so it might be sensible to join with other churches. Books and videos are also available and listed as above. Your local Baptist association may also be able to organise some training.

Protection of workers

The Guidelines are mainly about safeguarding children. Workers, too, need protection from both wrongful accusation and temptation. In training, leaders and workers should be made aware of actions which might be misunderstood, and situations which could render them vulnerable. The Good Practice guidelines, Appendix 3, p 28, give examples of attitudes and actions which will give protection to both children and workers.

Training our children to protect themselves

At an appropriate time, it will be necessary to talk with your children and young people about:

- the way the church is working to protect them;
- their right to be kept safe;
- access to the Children's Advocate as specified in Guideline 3, p 15.

This must be done sensitively and without generating undue fear or suspicion. It is best done in the context of the church's care for the whole child, possibly through the Advocate, who should be present sharing in the discussion. You may wish to inform parents of the church's policy, but children have the right to this information on their own account.

How much training you give children on self-protection and dealing with abuse will depend on your circumstances. You will need to explore whether they are being trained elsewhere, particularly at school. Many schools use Kidscape or a similar programme. Liaison is essential. You should never work on this in isolation. Any training done with children must be professional. If your children are not already being trained, and you intend to run a programme, parents should be involved in preparatory discussions.

Resource material for children is listed in Appendix 6, p 38.

Pastoral care

In a case of abuse

When, in a case of suspected abuse, the safety of the child has been assured, then the **worker's** feelings about the awfulness of the child's experience must be worked through. It is important for the church to create structures whereby **workers** can be counselled and supported. Similar help can be offered to **others surrounding the child** who may be damaged by what has happened. The church has a unique opportunity to offer a sensitive pastoral ministry to all who are involved. This may include the **abuser** and those close to him or her.

To your members

Members of your church and congregation who are, in their daily work, involved with cases of abuse must not be forgotten. They, too need the special support of your community.

To survivors

Training in abuse may bring to the surface suppressed memories of experiences from workers' own childhoods. They may be survivors themselves, who have never had the chance to come to terms with what happened in their own past. They may feel guilty about it. Specialist counselling will probably be needed, but the church community can provide a supportive environment. The guidelines for helping a survivor are similar to those for a disclosing child: listen, believe them, assure them they were not to blame. Begin where the person is, not with your own fears or preconceived ideas. Survivors are usually helped best by referral to professionals in this field. Appendix 6, p 39, gives suggestions of those who can help.

Safe from Harm, the Guidelines

*The 13 principles are listed in full in Appendix 1,
p26. The wording below has been altered slightly
to clarify their relevance to churches.*

It is the duty of each organisation working with children and young people to take appropriate action to apply the Guidelines to their own situation. Baptist churches differ widely in the way they work. Some employ paid staff, most rely entirely on volunteers. It is not possible to provide a standard formula for every church to follow. Each church, through its leaders and church meeting, will need to set up the necessary structures, but once this is done, you will know that you merit the trust of parents and guardians who give their children into your charge.

The Guidelines fall into five sections.

Section 1. Organising the church in order to protect children

> **Guideline 1. Adopt a policy statement on safeguarding the welfare of children**

A suggested policy statement is given on p 27. It may be adapted to suit your church's requirements, while retaining everything necessary for the implementation of the government recommendations.

It should be discussed and adopted by members at the church meeting, and displayed publicly. It must be known to all workers with children and young people.

Once a policy is written and published within the church, it would be good practice to reaffirm it each year at the annual church meeting or at an anniversary or covenant service. It is then placed at the heart of the community's spiritual life, and prayers can be offered for your children and workers. From time to time, you may need to amend it.

> **Guideline 2. Plan your work so as to minimise situations where abuse of children may occur**

There are many ways this can be done. The good practice guidelines set out in Appendix 3, p 28, or other appropriate procedures, should be observed by all who work with children and young people in the church. Each worker should receive a copy. These measures will also help to protect your workers.

> **Guideline 3. Introduce a system whereby children may talk to an independent person**

Access to such a person gives children and young people more rights and reduces the potential for undiscovered abuse. In a church, this independent person could have a wide role as a 'Children's Advocate'.

He or she should be someone not currently involved with children's work, but is a granny or grandad, a retired teacher, perhaps. Their function would be to establish contact with children and young people through existing organisations and groups, and be available to listen to whatever they wanted to share - it might be about school or church, faith or friendships. Within the confidence of this relationship, the child would be told that they could disclose abuse. The Advocate's wide ranging remit would reduce much of the fear or suspicion which could surround their role.

The independent person must be trustworthy; for greater protection, some churches may feel they wish to appoint two people. The advocate must be given appropriate training, and clear written guidelines as to what action to take if abuse is disclosed by a child. These guidelines should refer to the church's standard procedures for dealing with disclosure of abuse as specified in Guideline 12. Appendix 4, p 30, gives examples of procedures to follow in those cases.

You may wish to choose your own title for the independent person.

Section 2. Supporting staff in order to protect children

> *Guideline 4. Apply agreed procedures for protecting children to all workers*

It is not safe to assume that anyone can automatically be excluded from being a potential abuser. A person's good name or reputation should not be used to protect them. The steps you take to safeguard children, both in the way your work is carried out (Guideline 2) and in the appointment of staff (Guidelines 7-11), must apply to everyone who is in contact with children and young people, including the minister or others who work in the church. This is not the same as to treat each person working with children as being under suspicion: it is to take sensible steps to protect children, which everyone observes. Written acceptance of the church's policy statement on child protection would be a condition of service for all workers.

> *Guideline 5. Give all workers clear roles*

This prevents confusion which could conceal abuse. Most churches work with informal groups of voluntary helpers, but this does not reduce the need for clear roles and for accountability. So a job description would include:

- the person who supervises their work;
- the person whose work they will supervise (if any);
- a description of the work, with reference to the church's good practice guide;
- the duty to prevent abuse, with reference to the action to be taken if abuse is discovered or disclosed (Guideline 12).

An example can be found in Appendix 5 Form C, p 36.

A copy of the Good Practice guidelines and the agreed procedures (Appendix 3, p 24, and 3, p 30) must be given to each worker.

> **Guideline 6.** *Use supervision as a means of protecting children*

Each worker, however experienced, should have someone who oversees their work, for their own support as well as to protect the children. For the children's or youth work **leader**, it might be the minister or a deacon; the leader would do the same for other **workers**. It is always good practice for those given tasks to do by the church to meet regularly with its appointed representatives, to evaluate the work being done, and to pray and reflect. An outline of good practice in supervision can be found in Appendix 3, p 29.

Section 3. Choosing staff in order to protect children

"Is all this really necessary?"

As Christians, we trust one another, and it makes us uneasy if we suggest that we don't. Many church leaders feel they know their people so well that it is quite unnecessary to put them through these procedures. Others may be so short of adult help in children's work that they gratefully accept any offers that are made; to 'screen' volunteers places an extra burden on an over-stretched leadership. We have to weigh all this against our solemn duty to prevent unsuitable people working with children - which sadly can and does happen in churches, even with people we have trusted. A rigorous selection system may in itself act as a deterrent to potential abusers. Even when everyone is "checked out", though, we must never become complacent.

Once the procedures are set up, the church will use them as a matter of routine, and they will become part of the fabric of the community's life. They apply to churches of all sizes, and to regular and periodic helpers, paid and voluntary.

New opportunities

If no suitable people can be found, for whatever reason, it is better to have no separate children's and youth work than to appoint the wrong workers. It is better for churches to discuss imaginatively other ways of involving and nurturing children and young people than to stick rigidly to old patterns "because we've always done it like that". New ways need not be frightening, and might lead you into an exciting if challenging future. And remember, the Youth Ministry Office at Didcot is there to help you to talk through ideas and problems.

How, then, do we select and appoint workers?

If you think of it as being similar to employing someone in the 'secular' world, it will make more sense. The Guidelines clearly mark out the stages involved.

Stage 1

> *Guideline 7. Treat all would-be workers as job applicants for any position involving contact with children*

Either: ask the volunteer to fill in a short form, which will provide a personal record, including any previous experience they have had with children and children's work, including informal volunteering like babysitting. An example of a volunteer form can be found in Appendix 5 Form C, p 36.

Or: hold an informal interview with the recruit during which the details on the form are completed. Ask the would-be volunteer to check and sign it.

See also Guidelines 8 and 10.

Stage 2

> *Guideline 8. Gain at least one reference from a person who has first-hand knowledge of the volunteer's work with children*

In spite of the government recommendation, two references are recommended. If possible, visit one of the referees. Appendix 5 Form C, p 36, gives a suggested letter and reply form.

If the applicant has no experience of working with children, their referee should be a reputable person who can comment on their character and relationships with others. Vague or ambiguous replies should be followed up in person or by telephone.

A volunteer may be unsuitable for a number of reasons. A referee may suggest this, without being specific. Respect that confidentiality, and try to channel the person's offer into another area of the church's work.

Stage 3

> *Guideline 9. Explore the applicant's experience of working or contact with children in an extended conversation.*

If not already done in Stage 1, one or two people should talk with the applicant about his or her experience with, and expectations of, working with children. He or she should be asked to agree to follow the church's policy on safeguarding children's welfare, and to be prepared to undergo training. Although questions may be searching, the tone should be positive and supportive of both volunteer and children. At least one interviewer should be an experienced children's worker. In certain cases, it may be advisable to ask to see some form of identification, for example a driving licence or passport.

Stage 4

> *Guideline 10. Ask whether the volunteer has any conviction for criminal offences*

The legal position is that children's work is exempt from the Rehabilitation of Offenders Act 1974, as all convictions, however old, which relate to children and young people must be declared. Information about other criminal convictions should also be given, as these may be relevant to the suitability of the person.

In practice, this information is not easy to obtain. Police checks are not available to churches for their normal work with children. We rely on the volunteer answering the questions honestly, but only a small percentage of abusers is ever convicted. Habitual abusers admit to lying and scheming to gain access to children. This is where the references are so important, as is awareness of other signs of unsuitability, for example, if a person has moved frequently from one church to another.

A sample declaration is on the reverse side of Appendix 5 Form A, p 33.

Stage 5

Guideline 11. Make appointments conditional on the successful completion of a probationary period

---

If you now wish to appoint the volunteer to work with children or young people, you should agree an appropriate period during which he or she:

- is inducted into the work;
- begins training.

During this period, the supervisor should meet with the new worker regularly, and observe him or her with the children, to assess suitability. In the case of a short-term project, like a holiday club, the new worker should be supervised for the whole period. On an agreed date, the supervisor and the worker should meet to review the volunteer's performance, and the appointment should be confirmed or terminated.
The purpose of the probationary period is:

- to be assured that the worker is a suitable person, and not a potential abuser;
- to support her/him in this new work.

Because the worker is doing a valued job and the church is committing itself to support him or her, the appointment should be confirmed in a service of worship. At the completion of the probationary period, the members should publicly make a covenant with the worker, and the contract may then be signed. An example of a volunteer contract is in Appendix 5 Form C, p 36.

Section 4. What to do for child and worker if abuse is suspected or disclosed

---
Guideline 12. Agree and issue guidelines for procedure if abuse is suspected or disclosed

---

In all cases, a church must agree a procedure of consultation and referral. It is not the task of an individual or the church to investigate. For the protection of both children and workers, however, sensible steps should be taken on the road to referral.

If a child **discloses** abuse by someone outside the church, the person to whom it is disclosed should tell the child what steps they are taking, make notes as soon as possible after the disclosure, and report it to their church's Children's Advocate, or an appropriate leader (eg their supervisor or the minister). It should then be referred to an agreed outside agency (eg social services, NSPCC, police). If abuse is **suspected**, more detailed discussion and discreet observation need to take place before referral.

Guidance is given in Appendix 4, p 30 and 31, a copy of which should be given to all workers.

If abuse by someone in the church is disclosed or suspected, the procedure will be similar. It must be reported immediately to the supervisor, Children's Advocate and/ or an appropriate leader, who, after careful consideration, will make the appropriate referral.

Section 5. Training leaders and workers to protect children

> *Guideline 13. Train volunteers, supervisors and church leaders who make the policy decisions in the prevention of child abuse*

Besides personal preparation (p 13), all workers should be trained in:

- planning children's and youth work to prevent abuse;
- dealing with abuse when disclosed or discovered.

Training should also be organised for the children's work leader(s) in using supervision as a means of protecting children, and for the Children's Advocate.

The church's leadership (minister, deacons, elders) should consider training in effective policies to protect children, and discuss regularly the place of children and young people in the church.

Some new workers may go on to be children's and youth work leaders; to train them early will instil good habits which will remain with them, and become part of their standard working practice, to the benefit of children and young people in all our churches.

What about outside groups?

Many churches rent their premises out to other organisations working with children eg Tumble Tots, playgroups. In order to ensure they follow your standards of child care, it is recommended that a statement such as the following is included in any licence or agreement:

> **'The Licensee confirms that it is familiar with the Home Office Code of Practice *Safe from Harm*, have an understanding of it and undertakes to follow its guidelines in relation to work with children under 18.'**

Appendices

All appendices can be photocopied for church use. Many have spaces which can be filled in, whilst others are suggested outlines. Churches are free to adapt the wording to suit their own circumstances, as long as they remain in keeping with the spirit of the guidelines.

Paragraphs written in a different type-face are instructions, and can be omitted when photocopying.

Appendix 1: Guidelines

Safe from Harm: Summary of Recommendations
(Pub: Home Office, London 1993, ISBN 0 862529 93-X)

In order to safeguard the welfare of the children and young people in their charge, voluntary organisations should consider the issues raised by each of the following statements of principle and then, if they wish to do so, take any action which they deem to be appropriate in the light of their circumstances and structures, and the nature of their activities.

1. Adopt a policy statement on safeguarding the welfare of children.

2. Plan the work of the organisation so as to minimise situations where the abuse of children may occur.

3. Introduce a system whereby children may talk with an independent person.

4. Apply agreed procedures for protecting children to all paid staff and volunteers.

5. Give all paid staff and volunteers clear roles.

6. Use supervision as a means of protecting children.

7. Treat all would-be paid staff and volunteers as job applicants for any position involving contact with children.

8. Gain at least one reference from a person who has experience of the applicant's paid work or volunteering with children.

9. Explore all applicants' experience of working or contact with children in an interview before appointment.

10. Find out whether an applicant has any conviction for criminal offences against children.

11. Make paid and voluntary appointments conditional on the successful completion of a probationary period.

12. Issue guidelines on how to deal with the disclosure or discovery of abuse.

13. Train paid staff and volunteers, their line managers or supervisors, and policy makers in the prevention of child abuse.

Appendix 2: Policy Statement

Guideline 1

_ _ _ _ _ _ _ _ _ _ _ _ _ _*Church*

Policy statement on children, young people and the church

This statement was agreed at the church meeting held on _ _ _ _ _ _ _ _ _ _ _ _ _ _ _ _ _ _

It will be read annually at the church meeting held in the month of _ _ _ _ _ _ _ _ _ _ _ _ _
where progress in carrying it out will be monitored.

- As members of this church, we commit ourselves to the nurturing, protection and safekeeping of all, especially children and young people.

- It is the responsibility of each one of us to prevent the physical, sexual and emotional abuse of children and young people, and to report any abuse discovered or suspected.

- We recognise that our work with children and young people is the responsibility of the whole church.

- The church is committed to supporting, resourcing and training those who work with children and young people, and to providing supervision.

- The church is committed to following the Home Office Code of Practice *Safe from Harm* and adopts the guidelines and procedures published by the Baptist Union of Great Britain in its booklet *Safe to Grow*.

- Each worker with children and young people must know the recommendations, and undertake to observe them. Each shall be given a copy of the church's agreed procedures and Good Practice guidelines.

- As part of our commitment to children and young people, the church has appointed _ _ _ _ _ _ _ _ _ _ _ _ _ _ to be their Advocate (s). Their role will be regularly explained to children, and their names(s), address(es) and phone number(s) publicly displayed.

You might recognise the opportunity for your church formally to affirm the place of children and young people in your church's life, and add other statements. The Baptist Union's Charter for Children gives guidance. This is an example:

> **Children and young people are part of (or belong to) our church today. They have much to give as well as to receive. We will listen to them. As we nurture them in worship, learning, and in community life, we will respect the wishes and feelings of children and young people.**

Appendix 3: Good Practice guidelines for the prevention of abuse

Guideline 2

A. Good practice with children and young people

1. The church should ensure that:

● As far as possible a worker is not alone with a child where their activity cannot be seen. On church premises, this may mean leaving doors open, or two groups working in the same room.

In a counselling situation with a young person, where privacy and confidentiality are important, try to make sure that another adult knows the interview is taking place and with whom. If possible, another adult should be in the building, and the young person should know they are there.

● Ensure that access to the building is safe and well-lit.

2. You, the worker, should:

● Treat all children and young people with respect and dignity befitting their age; watch language, tone of voice, and where you put your body.

● Not engage in any of the following:
  - invading the privacy of children when they are showering or toiletting;
  - rough, physical or sexually provocative games;
  - making sexually suggestive comments about or to a young person, even in 'fun';
  - inappropriate and intrusive touching of any form;
  - any scapegoating, ridiculing, or rejecting a child or young person.

● Learn to control and discipline children without using physical punishment.

● Make sure another adult is present if, for example, a young child has soiled their underclothes and needs to be thoroughly washed.

● Not let youngsters involve you in excessive attention seeking that is overtly sexual or physical in nature.

● Not invite a child or young person to your home alone; invite a group, or ensure that someone else is in the house. Make sure the parents know where the child is.

● Not give lifts to children or young people on their own, other than for short journeys. If they are alone, ask them to sit in the rear of the car.

● Not share sleeping accommodation with children or young people if you take a group away.

B. Good practice with colleagues

If you see another member of staff acting in ways which might be misconstrued, be prepared to speak to them or to your supervisor about your concerns. Leaders should encourage an atmosphere of mutual support and care which allows all workers to be comfortable enough to discuss inappropriate attitudes or behaviour.

> *These measures will also protect workers from false accusation.*

This section should only be included on copies given to supervisors, and omitted from those given to workers.

Guideline 6

Good practice in supervision

- Meet with workers regularly to review and plan the work.

- Ask about working and personal relationships with the children.

- Take or create opportunities for observing the worker with the children.

- Ideally, keep a brief written record of the facts of each meeting and anything of note which you observed.

If the supervisor has any doubts about the worker's relationships, he or she should explore further by talking with him or her, then confidentially with other workers, and with the child concerned. The issue should not be dropped until the leader is sure there is no possibility of abuse.

Watch for any child receiving exceptional treatment, being highly favoured or treated unduly harshly.

Appendix 4: Procedures if abuse is disclosed or discovered

Guideline 12

The church and all its appointed children's and youth workers are committed to the protection of children from physical, sexual or emotional abuse.

Types of abuse

Physical	where children's bodies are hurt or injured.
Emotional	where children don't receive love and affection, may be frightened by threats or taunts, or are given responsibilities beyond their years.
Sexual	where adults (and sometimes other children) use children to satisfy sexual desires.
Neglect	where adults fail to care for children and protect them from danger, seriously impairing health and development.

Signs of abuse

The following *may* indicate abuse, but do not jump to conclusions. There could be other explanations.

Physical	unexplained or hidden injuries, lack of medical attention.
Emotional	reverting to younger behaviour, nervousness, sudden underachievement, attention seeking, running away, stealing, lying.
Sexual	pre-occupation with sexual matters evident in words, play, drawings; being sexually provocative with adults; disturbed sleep, nightmares, bedwetting; secretive relationships with adults or children; tummy pains with no apparent cause.
Neglect	looking ill-cared for and unhappy, being withdrawn or aggressive, having lingering injuries or health problems.

If abuse is disclosed or discovered:

● Do not delay.
● Do not act alone.
● Do not start to investigate.
● Consult with the person to whom you are responsible, the Children's Advocate within your church, or another person you trust.
● If appropriate contact * _____

The phone number is: _____

The person to speak to is: _____

If the child is in immediate danger, call the police. Their number is _____ or dial 999.

What to do if a child tells about sexual abuse

The following is a summary only, for reference. It is no substitute for training.

- Look at the child directly.
- Accept what the child says.
- Be aware that the child may have been threatened.
- Tell the child they are not to blame.
- Do not press for information.
- Reassure the child they are right to tell and you believe them.
- Let them know what you are going to do next, who you are going to tell and why, and roughly what will happen.
- Finish on a positive note.

- As soon as possible afterwards, make hand-written notes of exactly what the child said and the date and time.

What will happen next?

The process of professional involvement in cases of child sexual abuse will usually follow this course:

1. A strategy discussion involving Social Services, Police Child Protection team, other significant professionals and the person suspecting abuse or to whom the child had talked.

2. A decision will be taken as to whether an investigation is warranted; if so, it will then be planned.

3. The investigation may include:

   - an informal talk with the child;
   - a formal police (+/- social services) video recorded interview following disclosure;
   - medical examination;
   - preliminary family assessment.

4. If there is sufficient concern, a child protection conference will be held to decide the best course of action to protect the child and help the family. There may be criminal prosecution of the abuser.

Appendix 5: Forms

Form A - Guideline 7

＿ ＿ ＿ ＿ ＿ ＿ ＿ ＿ ＿ ＿ ＿ ＿ ＿ ＿ ＿ ＿ ＿ Church

Volunteer helpers form for work with children and young people

We ask all prospective helpers in children's and young people's work to complete this form. The information will be kept confidentially by the church, unless requested by an appropriate authority.

Name ＿

Address (including postcode) ＿

＿ ＿

Telephone no: Day ＿ ＿ ＿ ＿ ＿ ＿ ＿ ＿ ＿ Evening ＿ ＿ ＿ ＿ ＿ ＿ ＿ ＿ ＿ ＿

How long have you lived at this address? ＿ ＿ ＿ ＿ ＿ ＿ ＿ ＿ ＿ ＿ ＿ ＿ ＿ ＿ ＿

If less than 12 months, please give your previous address and the name of the church you attended.

＿ ＿

＿ ＿

Please tell us something of yourself - any special interests and skills you have, and previous experience of children or young people. Where appropriate name the church or group and the dates. (If there is not enough space, continue on another sheet.)

＿ ＿

＿ ＿

Have you any relevant qualification or appropriate training? ＿ ＿ ＿ ＿ ＿ ＿ ＿ ＿ ＿ ＿

＿ ＿

Are you prepared to undertake some (more) training?   YES/NO _(Please delete where applicable)_

Do you suffer, or have you suffered, any illness which may directly affect your work with children or young people? YES/NO

Reverse of form

References

In the space below, please give the names, addresses and telephone numbers of two people who know you well, who would be able to give a personal reference. Tell us their relationship to you.

1.   2.

Declaration

You will understand the great responsibility involved in working with children and young people, and the need to ensure their safety.

We therefore ask you to sign the following declaration.

Have you ever been convicted of a criminal offence, or are you at present the subject of criminal charges? (NB The disclosure of an offence may be no bar to your appointment.)

YES/NO

If YES, what was the nature of the offence? _

_ _

_ **Date** _ _ _ _ _ _ _

Signed _ **Date** _ _ _ _ _ _ _

All convictions must be disclosed, as the provision of the Rehabilitation of Offenders Act 1974 does not apply.

Form B: Letter and questionnaire to be sent to a referee - Guideline 8

_____ *Church*

Date

Dear

(Name of volunteer/worker) has offered to help with our children's/young people's work.

As you are probably aware, before we can accept any new volunteers/paid workers we must be sure that they are suitable. (Name) has given us your name as someone who can give a character reference.

I would be grateful if you could complete the enclosed questionnaire, which will be treated in the strictest confidence, and return it in the pre-paid envelope as soon as possible.

(Name) will mainly be working with (age) year olds, as (give a brief description of the work).

In commenting on the volunteer, please bear in mind that it is the church's duty to protect children from harm of a physical, emotional or sexual nature, and all volunteers are required to sign an undertaking to this end.

With thanks,

Yours sincerely,

(Minister/ Church Secretary)

Insert and delete where necessary

Reference Form

Private and Confidential

Name of volunteer _

What is your relationship with the volunteer?   Relative
Friend
Employer
Other (specify) _ _ _ _ _ _ _ _ _ _ _

_ _

How long have you known the volunteer? _ _ _ _ _ _ _ _ _ _ _ _ _ _ _ _ _ _ _

With your knowledge and experience of the volunteer, please comment on his/her suitability to work with children/young people. Please include comments about his/her honesty, reliability, health and experience of working with children/young people. (Continue over the page if necessary.)

Are there any other comments you would like to make about the volunteer?

Signed _ Date _ _ _ _ _ _ _ _ _ _

Form C: Volunteer Contract - Guideline 5, 6, 11

_ *Church*

Volunteer Contract

Name of worker _

We welcome you as _

You are joining a team which, together with the whole church, commits itself to the care and nurture of children and young people.

On behalf of the members of this church, we undertake to support you and your work, by prayer, by our interest, and by providing resources and training.

The person who will give you primary support is: _ _ _ _ _ _ _ _ _ _ _ _ _ _ _ _ _ _ _
He/she is there to discuss any matters of concern you may have.

The responsibilities of your job are: _

_ _

_ _

Once a year we will meet with you to talk about your work, and, if you wish to continue, we will discuss your development and training as appropriate.

Working with children and young people is a responsibility, but it also brings great rewards. We hope you will enjoy your work.

Signed _ Minister

Signed _ Church Secretary

Date _

One copy of this form should be retained by the worker, one by the person to whom the worker is responsible, one by the church secretary. If the job description changes, a new form must be completed.

The minister or other leader may wish to add a personal note of welcome, with an assurance of her or his availability for discussion.

Reverse of Form

Declaration

To be completed by the worker.

I understand the nature of the work I am to do with __ __ __ __ __ __ __ __ __ __ __ __ __ __ __ __

__ __

(Fill in the name and age range of the group.)

I have read the church's guidelines for safeguarding children. I understand that it is my duty to protect the children and young people with whom I come into contact. I know what action to take if abuse is discovered or disclosed.

Signed __ __ __ __ __ __ __ __ __ __ __ __ __ __ __ __ __ Date __ __ __ __ __ __ __ __ __

Appendix 6: Resources

A. Training for workers and church leaders

1. *Taking Care: A Church Response to Children, Adults and Abuse.* Written and edited by Hilary Armstrong. National Children's Bureau, 1991. Available from NCB at 8 Wakley Street, London EC1V 7QE.

   This pack contains background, training exercises, and a good list of resources. Suitable for 'distance learning' by churches, but the author advises groups using it to seek 'informed guidance' as well.

2. Professional training may be provided by:

   a) NSPCC, 67 Saffron Hill, London EC1N 8RS
   b) Spurgeon's Child Care, 74 Wellingborough Road, Rushden, Northants
   c) Kidscape, 82 Brook Street, London W1Y 1YG
   d) NCH Action for Children, 85 Highbury Park, London N5 1UD
   e) Diocesan Boards of Social Responsibility
   f) Social Services, or NHS Health Promotion Service (ask at your local health centre)

   To find out what is available, contact your local branch or project (if any) of a) - d), alternatively their main offices as above. For e) and f), contact your local office, which will probably be listed in the telephone directory.

3. 'Spectrum', the training course for youth workers, and 'Kaleidoscope' for children's workers, deal with abuse issues as part of generic training. For further details of these, contact the Baptist Union Youth Ministry Office.

B. Printed material for adults and children

1. NSPCC publish a series of separate information leaflets for parents, children and teenagers.

   In July 1994, the NSPCC commissioned a National Commission of Inquiry into the Prevention of Child Abuse. It will be taking evidence during 1994 and 1995, aiming to report early in 1996.

2. Independent Order of Foresters (IOF), Foresters Prevention of Child Abuse Fund UK, 36-38 Peckham Road, London SE5 8QR.

   They publish separate booklets on sexual abuse for general use, for parents, for children and for survivors, also a colouring book for young children.

3. Kidscape: write to Kidscape (Information) at the above address. Material for parents to use with children, and kits for use particularly in schools.

C.   Protection for Children

Leaflets from NSPCC and IOF, as above.

Kidscape have a programme of 'Good sense defence' for the young, through a kit for use with junior age children adopted by many schools, and a book and video for children based on 'The Willow Street Kids'.

D.   Emergency Helplines

Childline 0800 1111 (also handles adult calls).

NSPCC Child Protection Helpline 0800 800 500.

E.   Survivors

Most Rape Crisis Centres now offer counselling for women survivors. Local centres will be listed in the telephone directory. Childline and the NSPCC can put callers in touch with other sources of help. RELATE and the Samaritans have experienced and trained counsellors.

F.   Other Resources

There is a wide range of books available. Some of the above resources list the best in print at the time of publication.

Highly recommended for leaders and ministers is *Christianity and Child Sexual Abuse* by Hilary Cashman, SPCK 1993. This book also contains a comprehensive list of organisations set up to help children, victims, abusers and families.

Baptist Union Youth Ministry Office, PO Box 44, Baptist House, 129 Broadway, Didcot, Oxon, OX11 8RT. Tel 01235 512077, fax 01235 811537.